A Graceful View

Charles Sahr

First edition

ISBN (Paperback): 979-8-9913233-0-7
ISBN (eBook): 979-8-9913233-1-4

Published by Cardinal Hound Media Inc.

Cover design by Elisha Zepeda

Contents

Around The Pond
From The First Smile
The Final Day Of Youth
Immersed
From Here
Beach Day
Calm Of The Coldest Night
Tomatoes

AUTUMN

Breath Of Air
No Less
Lost In The Light
Marker
Tied Up
Just Listen
Artist At Work
Why Do I Write
Still
Work
Where To?
Justice
Value
Relaxing Stroll
Held Dear
My Wish
Who Am I?
Tis Time

WINTER

It Brings Me Back
Too Quiet
What Was Once
In The Silence Of The Night
Time
Overflow
Drifting
Fear Reigns
Hidden Scars

I.
SPRING

Harbinger Of Spring

Harbinger of spring

Is the airborne wedge of geese

On their flight back home

They return each fall

With new goslings and their mate

On their flight back home

That is correct for

The waterfowl have two true homes

One north and one south.

What a blessed bird

With vacation schedule

Already set in

Layers

Surface holds a clue to who you are

Showing signs of what is inside

Part rises to the surface for all to see

Most dwell deep within

Hidden to all but a few

Choice is yours to make

Under the surface

Lurks another you

Available only to trusted souls

Who you have chosen,

On the merit of their

Interaction with you

A Graceful View

Deeper in

You unravel just a little more of you

But this is not open

Except for very few

Who seem to think like you,

And after many years the door is opened

Deepest area

Is yours alone

Walls keep people out

And you in

Only you walk here

No one else enters in

Time comes when

Your world crashes in

Because one, you trusted

Decided to go another way

Opening your deepest level

To unbearable pain

Your prayers go up

Day after day

But you never lose hope

Or wander from the way

You were taught to live

Each and everyday

Seems easier to return

To who, you were

Because you treated everyone

Just the way you would want

Never throwing hate or pain

Outside of yourself

Wish the world could see

That hate tossed on people

Always makes a return trip

We, all are not the same

But we all walk in this world

So, lose the attitude and smile

A Graceful View

Someone needs that today

And let that person be you

Even though life is unfair

That you were born you

And they were born rich

But they have troubles, just like you

"How can that be?", you ask.

Because wealth hurts a soul

More than it helps

So, they only know rich

And do not know how to smile

But that is a layer they never will show

In life the happiest people you meet

Do not have much wealth at all

But they smile quick

And are always ready to help

When finished they seem to fade away

Because they are not living for today

Rather for the future

In the world above

Just A Prayer Away

First thing is to learn to laugh

Next learn how to make others laugh

Work hard at what you do

Pay no attention to what others do

Treat everyone with kindness

Even when they show you none

Help people whenever you can

And accept help when someone offers it

Believe in yourself

Because no one else will

Strive to take advantage of opportunity

Even if you have your doubts

Watch what people do

Not what they say they do

Seek out people, who are the same every day,

They will make a solid base

A Graceful View

Pray to the Lord each day

And thank the Lord for blessings each night

Time will come when loved ones are called

And without the Lord, you would walk alone

Shed tears when your heart hurts

Smile when your heart is light

In fact, smile whenever you can

Because your smile can help others too

Always be true to you

Whatever struggle or pain you go through

Because if you lose you

You are not worth anything to you

Pain will happen at times least expected

Heart will be broken by someone you love

Destiny and fate will have their way with you

But remember, the Lord is always a prayer away.

Trust In Us

Miles away I am proud to declare

There is a blessing we share.

Whether together or apart,

We share one heart.

You and I have became us,

A single unit of trust

So wherever I roam,

Part of me is always home.

One Day

Phrase heard growing up,

That never seemed to arrive.

Then suddenly it did appear,

But just as the celebration started,

It was over and done.

Seemed like an empty cup,

An image not worth the drive.

Okay it was finally here,

But no glory was imparted,

And it was over and done.

No longer backing up,

Forward I strive.

No longer with fear,

Life is now charted,

And soon over and done.

All Is Well

Life can be difficult at times

With a strong heart you proceed

Relying on the world to change

It doesn't, but you find a way to move forward

Along your way a friend slips and falls

You stop and turn to assist

Opportunity arises at that moment

You pass it by, then and it goes away

Now you wonder "what if"

From time to time

Never dwelling on it,

but always it is in memory.

Life itself is wonderful

So, you turn your focus to the beauty

Which comes to you each day

And a smile appears

A Graceful View

Pain and frustration hold on tight

But the joy of life trumps all

Now when you have a moment alone

For an instant all seems right.

Charles Sahr

Admired

One steps out from the crowd

Why is this one so proud?

What makes this one different?

Why was this one sent?

Perhaps life is just about luck

Not everyone boards the truck

Many labor long and hard with no reward

But only the chosen are called forward

I have often wondered as to why

I was never called up high

Perhaps it was just my plight

Or maybe my lack of foresight

I always wanted to be more

But I never led the store

Labor for me had its moments

Where success was seen in comments

A Graceful View

Never did I grasp the top

Nor I did not stop

My trying to stretch out

Though it did not work out

To those that won and the rest

Only time will attest

Whether the choice was right

Or just another error in this flight

Pitter Patter

On a spring morning,

rain falls in a slow

methodical pace

Beating out a steady rhythm.

Pitter – Patter

Drones on and on.

Daylight comes and goes,

But the rhythm presses on.

Slowly the song

enters the very soul

Of one, now awake

To the world and its ways

Gone is the illusion

Of a sunny forecast

Only dim hope remains

In the heart of one betrayed

Behind The Glass

I see the celebration

But can't get in.

Why was I not invited?

Was it something I did?

I might never know

I must move on

They had the chance

To welcome me in

But they neglected

leaving me behind the glass

Laughter and joy shared

With everyone but me.

I long for an invitation

To join in

Then the unexpected

Happens at long last

I am asked to enter in

And join in the celebration.

Odd thing occurred

Once I was inside

I saw someone

Crying behind the glass

I realized my error

And walk towards

I opened the door

And exit into the laughter

Inside that room

With doors of glass

A smile comes

I am where I should be.

Break A Rule

Life began following rules

Then one went down

And you waited on the storm

That never came

So, you took on a new approach

Going where you wanted

This felt wrong and good

At the same time

Before you knew it

You were lost in a maze

With choices made by you

Some right and others wrong

Then the moment came

When you had to set the rules

And realized you had lost

All guidance from your past

So, you started recalling rules made

By one, no longer around

You established a new norm

Rules new and yet the same

A Birthday Wish

From our first to our last

We try to enjoy our present and our past

Increasing candles on the cake

Requires a double take

Where did the time go?

When young it seemed to move so slow

Then after that last day of school

Each day sped up as a rule

Friends and family once around

Vanish and cannot be found

Journey becomes harder still

Though you push on until

You go alone on your own way

Leaving laughter and love to stay

In the many hearts you entered in

While giving this life a spin

The next edition is about to be

Hopefully I can still be me

Sharing love and laughter

Forever in the hereafter

Child Of Mine

Bond ever-present

Even when troubles arise

Clouding the path

No moment left alone

In younger years you resent

The judgment in my eyes

Worrying about my wrath

And how you will atone

Forever stuck in the help zone.

I just try to ease your path

One day you will realize

That I have only good intent

So, for now just hold the phone

And let go of your pent-up wrath

Try and see the world thru my eyes

Hopefully you will see what I meant

Charles Sahr

You were a gift heaven sent

That changed my life path

So, it should come as no surprise

That our hearts beat to the same tone

Loved my job as a parent

Hoped you found the right path

In my heart you are until my demise

Then you will walk on, still not alone

Though you might feel alone

I watch you still with angel eyes

No longer able to guide your path

I just keep praying for you

You will never be left alone

For even when my body dies

My spirit is with you

Watching over my one heaven sent.

Zig Zag

Two steps forward, one to the right

Now you are ready for the night

Place money on skills attained

Nothing will be gained

If you choose to play it safe

One step backward, two to the left

Your skills are bereft

So, regroup and try anew

Let nothing defeat you

Nothing gained by being safe

Spin on your heels

Like the way it feels

Different day at hand

Let's kick this old stand

Safe is the other way

Charles Sahr

Turn and twist

Leave them amidst

The ones once held high

Whose laws lived by

Now is time to play.

The Smile Returns

Life has its share

Of ups and downs

Loss of any kind hurts

Causing the spirit to sink

With no time to spare

One comes to remove the frowns

Easing all that hurts

Bringing you back from the brink

Great to see your smile back

To where you once were

Road of pain is long

But it is finally beat

So now back on track

Emerging from the blur

After a long sad song

Life again is sweet

Memory tries to hang on

But you are cried out

Time to dance again

And feel your heart sing

Impact of one gone

Which had knocked you out

Has had its reign

Time once again to sing

To Those Lost

Each of you are missed

By all, who love you

Sorry, that in your final hours

We couldn't be at your side

Though death is a solo journey

It helps when you can say goodbye

Thanks for the love you shared

With all of us lucky enough

To be around you on your journey

Hopefully you are at peace

After fighting this

You are remembered

And reside safe in our hearts

Forevermore

Doorstep

Here I sit waiting

On a friend, who never came

Why? I'll probably never know

Raindrops begin to fall

So, I head inside

After a few hours the rain stops

So, I sat back down on the step

Waiting once more

Then a flicker of blue caught my eye

A blue jay had flown by

Then a squirrel sprinted past

With bushy tail behind

Then he stopped and looked around

Checking to see if he was safe or not

A Graceful View

In an instant the squirrel ran off

Leaving me waiting on the doorstep

After a few minutes my neighbor's cat

Came by and brushed against my leg

Purring as he made his pass

Time to go in for the night

Wonder why my friend never came

Glad though for the time spent outside

On the doorstep

Enjoying the world

Charles Sahr

Wren

A little songbird

Often overlooked, but heard

And enjoyed by all

Loud and complex songs

Composed and sung by this bird

Make the world happy

A strong voice always

Unassuming plumage hides

Body not the voice

Listen for their tune

From the treetops to the ground

When hiking the trail

Intense

Racing pulse,

Deep breathing

For a reason

Yet undisclosed.

After a brief eternity

Calm again.

Cause known

Now to all

Shocking many.

A relationship

turned sour

after many years.

Charles Sahr

How one deals

with betrayal

Where love once ruled

Sleep now a fight

not often won,

But it does occur.

How to proceed

With a Life not shared

Tears solve nothing

but show remorse

Over an oath broken

By just one

Time heals all wounds

Often said, but is it true

Walking solo now

Through my daze

The struggle forward

Alone is tough

A Graceful View

Finally, after years

Broken heart beats

A little faster

New love found!

No longer on

The path alone.

From Dust To Dust

I walk where my ancestors walked

The dust beneath my feet

Was tread upon by them

The dust beneath my feet

Was between their toes

As they walked barefooted

Dust became mud in the rain

Once dry it was dust once more

My footsteps in the dust

Beneath my feet

Will one day be invisible to all

But I have walked this path

And moved the dust beneath my feet

Time will keep moving on

Only memory of me may be

That I too walked upon this dust

A Graceful View

My laughter will pass one day

When my family is all gone

But always someone

Will walk where we walked

Upon the dust beneath our feet

So, you are never truly alone

Because there is just one world

To have dust beneath your feet.

Time Will Tell

What will surface?

What will remain hidden from view?

Some think they know what will be,

But at best it is a guess

Based on what?

Intuition or clairvoyance?

Don't tell me you know,

Because frankly you just can't.

I hope whatever does break through

Is a good example of what, should be

World needs some help these days

For most think so small

Too many complain

Little do anything to help

Unless of course they benefit from it

Which means of course that we go backward

A Graceful View

Best ideas come from the simple people

Who labor long and hard

No one notices them and fewer care

Unless of course they can benefit from it

Sad world we live in

And it is getting darker day by day

Still we push on, hoping for a moment

When an actual leader sees what is going on

Takes a moment to thank all who labor

And then stretches out an arm to help

No one alone can change the world

But together we can

Time will soon tell

Whether this world will go on

Or fade into the blackness

I hope for light, but I am only me

II.
SUMMER

Summer Daze

Hot sun beating down

Sand in between your toes

Relaxing with a beer or two

Now this is something to smile for

Hearing the surf roll in and out

On a sun kissed day

Troubles just slip away

This is what life should be about

Days that mend the soul and more

Simply rejuvenating you

Tossing aside your woes

Slowing the pace of life down

Charles Sahr

Wearing flip flops and napping

In the heat of the day

Good life brings an easy laugh

Waves white capping

At the close of another day

Another beautiful photograph

Sunsets are a thing to savor

Bringing breezes in to cool

The quiet hours of the night

Life takes on a different flavor

Only missed by a common fool

For this is living life right.

Beach House

You can hear the noise of the tide coming in

And feel the warm breeze on your cheeks

This is the gift of living close to the beach

Morning walks along the beach

Feeling the sand shift in between your toes

Choosing sea shells brought in by the tide

Across a stretch of sandy beach

There is a damp odor that prevails through the breeze

Salt air fills the lungs and relaxes the inner soul

Midday the beach is much the same

But the sun beats down with intensity

So, you dash into the ocean to cool off

The breeze though reduced, is still there

But not enough to cool you in the heat of the day

So after just a little while you return

To the beach house for lunch and a cool drink

A nap is also on your agenda

But looking out from the huge porch to the ocean works too.

Charles Sahr

Evening finds the beach less crowded

As everyone carts off their towels and toys

To get dinner and treat the sun damage of the day

One or two fishermen arrive to steal from the sea

Standing on the ever-shifting sand

Casting out their lines to bring home a meal

The sun begins to fall in the sky

And the tide starts to roll in

Erasing footprints from the day

Night brings calm to the beach

And a cooler breeze that comforts the soul

You sit on the large front porch

To enjoy the smell of the salt air

And laugh at the fun shared that day

The moon lights up the beach just enough

To entice a slow walk along the sandy beach

Care and concern constant in another setting

Simply seem not to exist in this environment

Love the serenity of my beach home.

Blank Canvas

How intimidating it can be

To have a blank canvas staring back at you.

Then again how exciting

To be able to create the scene

You have somewhere in your head.

To start the process, you must add the paint

And begin putting it on the blank canvas

Start simple with a base coat

Then accentuate with colors chosen

In the space inside your head.

Now take a moment and close your eyes

And see the picture of what you want it to become

You are ready now to begin in earnest

Paint with all of you

Not just the little brush you use.

Charles Sahr

Something doesn't feel right

Pause for a moment and regroup

A creation doesn't need to be hurried along

Time is required to get it right

So, when you know how to fix your issue, do it.

Almost done the canvas explodes with color

But is it what you wanted at the start?

Pause again, and take it all in

If it all looks right to you

Add the finishing touch, your signature.

Crayons

Diversity in action,

Each different, yet able to blend.

All driven toward a single goal,

Taking a concept to completion.

No one stronger or weaker,

Just a team at work.

Impressive to see in action,

A unified group of contributors,

Focused on a single goal.

One force not in competition,

No one stronger or weaker,

Just a team at work.

Charles Sahr

Achieving astounding results,

No one more dominant,

No one more oppressed.

A model of perfection,

Focused only on the end,

Rather than each other.

Lessons to be learned,

From the melded group,

Are varied and plentiful.

Embrace the differences,

Drive on and defend,

Rather than destroy each other.

Creativity

Not something that is always easy

It can be a struggle if it wants to be

Having a focus group helps to enhance

The drive in each to share the dance

Each input forms a new idea, spurring imagination

Often guiding one to their destination

Those who choose not to play a part

Are left to just develop what's in the heart

Neither choice is right or wrong

Both will share your inner song

The world needs creativity everyday

To enhance the memories of yesterday

Choice is made inside of you

As to which you want to do

Either way another might help you

And you might help them too!

Charles Sahr

Last comment on this subject

Be aware of who you infect

They will need your input

For it contributes to their output.

.

Composed

Pulse races as thoughts drift back to younger years

Many loved ones have passed on

Now the realization hits, that time is running out

So, anxiety level raises to an all-time high

You struggle to get beyond it, but it requires some help

From outside sources, for a time it seems unbeatable

Then almost as sudden calmness returns

As a younger being, did I have these fears,

When loved ones started to pass on?

Maybe I thought time would not runout

Or perhaps I just didn't want to deny

That my younger version would ever need any help

Guess youth tends to not dwell on the inevitable

Just enjoying all that happens when the world turns

Charles Sahr

Now as time dwindles down for me

I just want to leave a lasting mark

That will keep a pleasant memory

In the hearts of ones I loved

Time will one day erase the memory of me

But I hope I will always be

In the hearts of ones I loved

Treasured in their memory

Daunting Task

Living in a world that changes each day

Never knowing what is coming next

Happy for good things that happen

Sad for bad things when they occur

Tendency is to keep pushing through

Works on all but the most challenging days

Then tears help, but the heartache holds on

Days pass slowly by, until the heart smiles again

Try and keep your focus on the positive

It will help you through the negative

Praise the one above always

Even when darkness tries to overwhelm

Help others without expecting anything in return

You will be paid back in full

Lastly thank the one above

For yet another day in this world

Overwhelmed

Life has a way of overwhelming

Mundane simple tasks grow

Into insurmountable obstacles

Pressure to achieve

Becomes a sidebar

As life turns into a fierce battle

Nights bring on sleeplessness

As you struggle to maintain being you

What causes the upheaval?

Uncertain, perhaps just life itself

Forward you must persist

Even though your heart

Isn't in it

Improvement will come

If you persist

But it will not be easy

But it will be worth it

Bedside Table

A catchall for things past

Holding treasures fast

At times almost overrun

Yet never truly done

Upkeep a dreaded chore

For questions just pour

What to keep and what to toss

Time deciding is a loss

So how can I downsize

The clutter before my eyes

Many attempts tried

But still on the losing side

Soon the table will overflow

So, I'll just stack and stow

Putting memories in a pile

Until I have awhile

Charles Sahr

To thin the stack amassed

Will be a task unsurpassed

By the unorganized me

Will I ever be free

Just a question posed

For one so truly hosed

By indecision on the way

To make clutter go away

Overwhelmed, help I finally seek

And then within a week

The table is nearly clear

And I have just one fear

That the clutter will reappear

Take over and confirm my fear

Never will I be able

To keep clear the table.

A Graceful View

A different thought takes hold

Perhaps all things be told

The table might never be free

For it tells the tale of me

Forever

Word seldom used into today's world

Structures once built to house a business

Vibrant and alive for decades

Torn down after many years

Pyramids still stand

But the building is now gone

Why can't forever be

Is it to live on

Only in memory

Pictures will retain much longer

For we too are not here forever

Wish it were not the way

And structures could stay

Oh well tears fall

And another day comes

What was once alive

Now a pile of rubble

Hope the new replacement

Will be around for years

A Graceful View

Doubtful that will be

For progress must be made

Move on is now the way

And so it goes

Charles Sahr

Around The Pond

Summer breeze feels good after it dances over the pond

Bending the cattails over

hitting your face as you sit holding your pole

No fish yet, but they will come

Grab another beer from the cooler

Then lay back on the tall grass

Tip your hat over to cover your eyes

Keeping the fishing line between your fingers

This is the life

Just about to drift off you feel your line tighten

The fish fights hard but soon his battle is done

And he is added to the stringer

You toss your line back in after adding a new worm to the hook

You stretch back out and this time you doze off

Then again you feel your line tighten

What a nice slow-paced routine on a summer day

Around the pond.

From The First Smile

From across the room

A smile caught my eye

Then something happened

And I felt my heart stir

What was I to assume

I had to find out why

And what had happened

When I felt my heart stir

Finally, I crossed the room

To ask and find out why

Was I finding love

Or was it just my wishful heart.

As I crossed the room

To find out exactly why

And what I was thinking of

With my once broken heart

Charles Sahr

Then the moment came

Together we sat

And it soon became

A long relaxing chat

Now the smiles are shared

For together we walk

A couple paired

Soon after our first talk.

The Final Day Of Youth

All your friends were there

Laughing and unaware

That moments like this were about to fade

From sunlight into the shade

This was our last time to share a smile or a tear

Most would walk on alone from here

Looking back, I still have one crazy request

That I could relive just one moment from our best

I would love to see everyone

Back in the joy of that moment, when we thought we won

In truth, however we just said, "Goodbye"

To our youth and our friends, who stood by.

Charles Sahr

Walking forward from that day

Has had its ups and downs along the way

Friends have passed, and tears shed

Joy has also been, and all things said,

Time spent with friends from days past

Helps to make the memories last

Time will always march on

But what remains after we are gone

Is it the joy that we brought?

To others who shared our lot

In this place of tears and laughter

Just a little stop before the hereafter.

Immersed

Absorbed in each day's offerings

Often to an overwhelming amount

Moments race by

Attempts to capture

Fall far short

Best way to proceed

Immerse yourself

In the moment

Worrying not about

What might transpire

Just savoring

What is

There will be sorrow,

Stress and more

No matter

Joy will appear

And peace will be

Too short a time

Is allowed

Charles Sahr

So immerse yourself

And let go

From Here

Simple phrase that tells a lot about you

In truth, it only tells your starting point

Others disagree saying that it tells much more

They are wrong, because each decision made

Changes you inside and out

Your demeanor might be formed early

But that is only one step in your journey

So, who are you then?

No one has been with you through it all

Some have walked along for awhile

But the journey in all truth is yours alone

Answer is simple, "You are you."

That is all you are and have ever been

And will ever be.

Charles Sahr

My hope is that you have shared laughter,

Love, and more with those you cherish

Been kind and helpful

Along the way

Most of all I hope

You will leave behind a smile

When they recall, when you were here

Beach Day

Brilliant blue sky above a pristine beach

Vision of beauty in the mind's eye

Waves slowly cresting as they roll in

Is this not the most pleasant place on earth?

Body relaxes as you bake in the sun

Stress drifts quickly away

Perfect day to lay out on the beach

Just enjoying all that I see

At peace and ready to begin

Another day on the beach in rebirth

Creating a new spirit of fun

To see me through each day.

Charles Sahr

I pray but do not preach

But we, all should adore thee

For allowing us to settle in

On your gift of this earth

To live and enjoy in the sun

Savoring the moments of each beach day.

Goals now seem within reach

My spirit feels like it is free

Ready at last to begin

An effort to increase my worth

Donating and giving back has begun

Sorry, I have so little time to repay.

Calm Of The Coldest Night

Ever listened to the howling of a winter wind

Coming across the fields unimpeded on its path

Poking your head out of the door to feel it's might

Shutting it quickly upon feeling the chill upon your face.

There is a calm that comes from the chilling wind

For almost no one will venture into its path

So, all you hear on a windy night

Is the roar of the wind that keeps all in their homeplace.

Not a creature stirring until the winds rescind

Leaving just the destruction of its' wrath

Animals poke their heads out after the terror of the night

To explore what food is now available in the space

All seem glad that somehow, they were left behind

After the night when the wind was on the warpath

Bunnies hop, squirrels climb and a groundhog even finds sunlight

The world has been rearranged and had a change of pace

Charles Sahr

As night falls and another day is cast behind

I smile and enjoy the aftermath

Of an extremely windy night

Now it is time for me to readjust my pace.

Tomatoes

Fruit or vegetable

Who cares, as long as they taste good?

I used to think Beefsteak was the top of the heap

Then I had a Cherokee Purple

And I found my new love.

Signal that summer has started

Are garden fresh tomatoes

At every vegetable stand, grocery store

And, of course right off the vine

You eat them in salad, right off the vine,

cut up with a little salt or sugar,

Layered on a sandwich with only mayonnaise

Or with bacon, lettuce and mayo.

You smile when you eat them

And laugh when they squirt on your brand new shirt

You can eat them almost daily until you can't

Then you drive by the vegetable stands

Looking for the last remnants of the season

And finally after a week or so, you realize

Charles Sahr

The tomatoes are done for the season

And you wipe back a tear

Because summer is at an end

III.
AUTUMN

Breath Of Air

Pressure mounts daily

Past fixes no longer work

What is the new fix?

No one seems to know

Worse yet our leaders sense it

And use it on us

Some see only hate

Which is which? Depends on you

Crumbling walls fall

Brother against brother

Same as when the world began

Peace no longer here

Will we throw away

All the beauty or hide it

For our own pleasure?

Charles Sahr

Time will reveal all

To a new and calmer world

Not the one today

No Less

Searching for a path to follow

      Starting at a point not yet there

All promises of joy seem hollow

      And steps toward go nowhere

      Gain some insight from the test

Of going in a direction chosen

      Hearing chatter from the rest

            Who in part are frozen

Can hopes be reached

      Or will failure reign

            Future breached

    Yet still no gain

Life has been grand

      Years later confess

Though never held the upper hand

      Just survived more or less

Charles Sahr

Dreams still come and go

But pass quickly through

Even though

They continue to grow.

Lost In The Light

Direction comes

Even in the dark

Light can illuminate your path

But you need to steer

For like a ship

You must hold your course

Or never reach your intended destination

At times the light seems to blind

The eyes and soul

Persist and hold your heading

It will serve you well

As you strive to attain your goal

Across the great expanse

That is this world

Heart strains and muscles ache

Giving up will never do

No one can finish your trek

Charles Sahr

For the goal you strive for

Is yours and yours alone

Once in your possession

Reach out to a further destination.

Light reveals, and dark conceals

Either way you choose your path.

Marker

Holds a record of their name,

Marital status, birth and death

In a field full of other markers

That serve the same purpose

Few come to visit, more than once or twice a year

Some do not come at all

Others come every year or two

The stone holds nothing for most

Only a reminder of someone

But lacking what is missed most

A kiss, a hug, a laugh or a smile

So, why do we have this memorial spot

The one passed is not returning

Eventually no one will remember

Who the person was and worse

How they laughed, what they built,

Or even who they loved.

Charles Sahr

I first visited the marker

One year after the terrible event

That tore my heart in two

I walked up to the marker and knelt

Talking to the stone as if it could feel my pain

I prayed then for a miracle for one moment more

With the one laid there, but it was not to be

I felt the presence of the one passed

Then I wept the tears of one

Missing the love of the one taken

By the one above.

Then I realized they were not here

In any shape or form

The tears calmed my spirit

Reading the dates and the name

Brought other memories back

And I cried again

Then I turned and said, "Goodbye"

To the one, I will forever treasure

A Graceful View

Markers do serve a purpose

Some embrace it as that special place

Where they feel connected

To the one who has gone on

Some don't want to be reminded

Of one they loved so they stay away

Others simply do not care

And feel nothing from the simple stone

That marks the grave site

I see it as a mourning spot

That simply helps us past

The sorrow and loss we feel

So, I believe it helps us along

But that is my thought alone.

Charles Sahr

Tied Up

Does this reflect me

Am I tied up inside or

Just stressed by life

I remember when

My soul was much more at peace

And I smiled more

Crazy how it goes

In one direction and then

Off the chart it goes

A new course now set

And the rate full-speed ahead

No thought of return

Today will pass on

But lessons learned will remain

Living on forever

A Graceful View

In the beating heart

Within my chest hidden deep

Safe always with me

Charles Sahr

Just Listen

To wind as it whistles through the trees

Growing into a breeze

That at times in spring can make you sneeze

Oh, but how it can make you feel at ease

Birds sing their catchy tunes as they drift along

Filling the woods with a soothing song

This is where I wish I could stay for long

Enough to feel, that at last I belong.

City sounds are a little rougher than nature

But they help to paint the total picture

And guide our way into the future

They mold us into something less pure

Silence can also inspire

But sitting and listening to the crackling fire

I will absolutely, never ever tire

Of the sounds that transpire

A Graceful View

Morning sounds in the country

Seem to almost always wake me

While sounds in the city

Do the same, but as hard as they try to be

They fall short in the comforting way

Which the country noises start the day.

There are more high notes that play

Upon the morning breeze each day.

So, if I had my choice of where to be

My choice is super easy

I wish to spend my mornings in the country

Where the calming sounds of morning be.

Charles Sahr

Artist At Work

Returning color to the world

After a few months away

Painting trees in blossoms

Using many different colors

On your brush

Purple, red and white

To name just a few

Flowers also are being painted

In a vast array of colors

The world is grateful

For the new artwork

It recalls beauty of years past

But there seems to be a new vigor

In the brush strokes

For the colors are making

The spirit dance again

Very much needed at this time

For all need a new view

On the canvas

That is our world

Why Do I Write

A fair question

Maybe because I want to tell a story

Or perhaps I just want others to enjoy

Moments that I ran through

And wish I hadn't

Might be I just want to look back

At my own piece in this puzzle

We call life

I didn't really think about why

Until I heard other's stories

Which, seemed better than mine

Which, is great for them

Really do not think it is about my ego

Could be a little

No, it is more than that

At least I hope it is

Charles Sahr

Everyone writes from their own perspective

Catching things that others miss

And missing things others have caught

Guess I just want my version

To be out there in the open

hopefully it gives others joy

still I am happy for this gift

God blessed me with

Life has a way of limiting

moments available

To just enjoy the journey

Too often the pace of life

Demands most of your energy

Hopefully my writing

Does at least one thing

And makes you want to slow it down

A Graceful View

So, you can look around

Take stock of the beauty

That surrounds us all

At all times

And allow you to enjoy those around you

While they can walk with you

It will help you through

When you walk alone.

Charles Sahr

Still

I still hear her voice

Though gone for many years

My heart still holds her memory

Her voice resonates in my ears

Once she combed my hair

And wiped away my tears

At night she would talk to me

Calming my childhood fears

I am closer now to the end

When I can again hold her close

Until then I will send

My love in prayers up to her

My heart will never fully mend

Until I wrap my arms around her

Wish, hope, and pray in the end

She'll still smile when she sees me, once again!

Work

Some want to do it

Others prefer to avoid

No way right or wrong

How to pay the bills

With either choice that is made

That is the problem

Many choose to work

Some take a different path

And stay home instead

Of those that stay home

They struggle with bills and debt

In the end who cares

Our mission here done

Our life is measured by one

Who looks only for love shown

Charles Sahr

Where To?

Question asked

no answer given

For I know not where my path will go

Thought I did at one point in life

But I was proven wrong

I no longer try to pick my way

Now instead I rely on feelings

Held inside my heart

Am I right to do so?

Not sure

But it is no longer my dilemma

To pick and choose a path

Instead I pray

And hope for guidance from above

Silly you might say

But what in life do we control?

Our thoughts, hopes and dreams

Maybe but if fate swoops in

Removing one of our choices we need

A Graceful View

We have no option

But to change from that path

We can choose to mourn forever

Or to find a way past the pain

So, simply put our control

Is limited to our eyes and

How we choose to view the world.

Justice

In, reality is

Not here except in theory

Hope it arrives soon

World needs it badly

But it is not seen nor heard

Anywhere on Earth

At least it appears

To be that way in the world

There has, to be hope

The trend seems to be

Hate taking over all things

Not true, sure seems so

It is not one place

That harbors hate but many

Though we try to stop

A Graceful View

Solution hidden

Or is no one looking for

A way to stop it

Sad that we hold hate

Deeper in our hearts than love

I pray that it stops.

I promise to love

Move hate to where it can't hide

And replace with love

I pray I am not

The lone one praying for it

Because we need it

To the one above

I ask for help removing

Hate in all the world.

Charles Sahr

World is in crisis

Just holding onto the hope

That you will help us.

Praise your name always

This is beyond our power

Only you can resolve.

Wish it were not so

Give us the strength to hang on

Till your will is done

Value

All have value

Each differ

But all have value

Not the monetary sense

But the spiritual sense

In life,there are moments

When help is needed

Who steps up to help?

Those with real value

They transcend this life

Making world better

Carrying it on to the next

Money and power

Fall away

When called from above

Only thing of value left

Simple it is Love

Live your life with love

This world might not see it

Charles Sahr

But in the one above

It will shine brighter

Than any star below

Relaxing Stroll

Path through the woods

Takes you from sunlight

To shade and back

Leaves on the trees shake

As the breeze says hello

To even the darkest spots

Creatures big and small

Meander in the dark

Trying to safely eat and drink

Without being noticed

Footsteps heard to the right

A deer beautiful and fast

Kicks into high gear

Once your head turns to see

You stay quiet hoping to find

More beauty along the way

From high above is a sound

When a squirrel jumps

From one tree to another

Charles Sahr

Such a high flying daredevil

No signs of any nerves or fear

Breeze picks up and trees bend

Ahead a hare races across

The well worn path

Zigging and zagging

Disappearing into a stack

Of fallen trees and brush

What a beautiful walk

Through the woods

From above the trees

I hear a crow cawing

Claiming territory

Alas the stroll ends

I walk thru the front door

Leaving beautiful nature behind

Held Dear

Memory latches on to items from the past

At times it can overwhelm and even take over

Tears help to ease the pain of days never to return

There is a long shadow cast

By things that we wished, we could do over

There is no energy present however to burn

Bad memories from where they hold fast

Good memories will always hover

From both forms we forever learn

That what we have held dear

Will not leave us to walk alone

Unless by our own choice we choose to

Heart still feels the emotion of days we fear

And the joy of days when we once set the tone

Moving on is rough, but in time we do

We will progress through it all, that is clear

But no one can replace one neath a headstone

So, enjoy moments shared, for too soon it shall take you.

Charles Sahr

Remember the kiss of yesterday

Feel the love of one once here

Then wipe away that single tear

Memories good or bad will never go away

They might shift to the background where

The fog sets in a little and they are a little worse for wear

Then something will trigger it to come back one day

Names and faces will come back and be there

Triggering, even more to reappear.

My Wish

In life, my wish has always been simple

Not for possessions, wealth, or fame

Only that my children surpass me, in all things

While still being kind, generous, and loving

My wish, but it must be their choice

For my input is already in

They are the future

While I am the past

May their choices in life

Be much better than mine

Hope they look to the One above

As I have in times of struggle

Either way their lives go

It is their choice alone

My guidance is kept quiet

Until they ask, not before

Charles Sahr

I love watching them succeed

And cry when they stumble

They will always be my children

But their life is theirs alone

Who Am I?

Am I, who people think I am?

Or am I, who people want me to be?

Well both views have merit, however I am just me.

Does that mean, I am just me inside

Or does that bleed over to the outside?

Enough questions?

Here is my view,

To myself, I am just me

To others, I am who they see me to be

Relationships and proximity to me

Can change the me you see

Or at least your view of me.

Charles Sahr

To close this little query into who I am

Let me say that my heart will not ache

Nor my feelings be hurt

If your perception of me.

Is not who, I see me to be.

For I am after all, just me.

Most important thing to me

Is not what you see

But who, I see myself to be

I will always work on improving me

But who you see is and will always be

Just your version of me.

Tis Time

What is done, is done

Now we must cast hate aside

And unite as one

Not a choice to make

But an essential need now

For all to survive

Stay apart all passes

Stand together all remains

A future is born

IV.
WINTER

It Brings Me Back

Christmas in our home always included baking

Most of our time was spent cookie making

Mom had a few recipes from her side

And Dad had a few that he made with pride

I can still smell the cookies baking

And I have passed on this joy of cookie making

To my children, and hopefully to the next generation

So, even now at Christmas I have the sensation

That Mom and Dad are in the kitchen baking

And letting me help in the cookie making

I realize that it now is only me

But what a connection to my family

So, next year when I am in the kitchen baking

Enjoying the art of cookie making

I will take a moment to breathe in the smell

And savor the memory of baking with Mom and Dad as well.

Charles Sahr

Too Quiet

Alone and afraid

But safe and secure

away from all

who can infect

Worth the price

Depends on you

your health

and your outlook

Like the quiet

but it gets old

after a few days

depressing the spirit

A Graceful View

Interactions needed

Between People

in daily life

Without them

life is not the same

Hope this crisis

Passes quickly

Because I miss

Spending time with you

Charles Sahr

What Was Once

Once treasured and protected,

The tree grew strong and tall.

After many years it was infected,

And all braced for the fall.

Waiting for what seemed like years,

Until, finally it fell with a deafening thud.

The dust of impact creating a haze,

Covering what was once in forest mud.

All those years of life now over,

Leaving behind a stump to hold its place.

Serving as its headstone in the clover,

A long full life ended in place.

Yes, Once mighty and strong,

It basked in the glorious sun.

Then a simple bug came along

In The Silence Of The Night

Now at night sometimes I hear

A song from yesterday playing

Is it in my head alone?

Or is the tune being played

Somewhere in the space between

Heaven and earth?

In the dead of night when silence rules

I hear my mother's soothing laugh

And though I know she has passed on

I still turn hoping to see her once again

Then the silence returns

And I drift off with a smile on my face

In the morning I awake with the smile

That came to me that night

When my mother came across

From the place where she now resides

So that I, her oldest son

Would awake with a smile on his face

Charles Sahr

You might not believe in miracles

But I do, because I have heard my mother laugh

In the silence of the night

She visited once before

Right after she had passed

I know, because I heard her footsteps

Walking round the bed

Where, my young son slept

Now as my father's time dwindles

And he has trouble remembering

I hope and pray my mother's voice

Is calming him

In the growing fog

That now clouds his memory

I still listen for other sounds

That travel in the silence of the night

But that isn't how it happens

For they seem to come unannounced

When they are least expected

But probably most needed.

Time

Always there, but ever changing

Quiet and calming,

loud and obnoxious.

Never the same, yet always there

Morning comes and goes in an instant,

Then night takes over and passes on.

Savor the moments that you have,

Before they vanish

Nothing stays forever.

If I had one wish,

It would be to hold one moment

From when I was young, forever.

Charles Sahr

Overflow

Occurs when capacity is reached

Only option, overflow the boundary

That kept all contained

Now all is shared

Despite effort to retain

All within a reservoir

Outside of the boundaries

It spreads engulfing all

No longer limited in reach

It can destroy most areas

But it brings other areas

New Life

A Graceful View

Within boundaries, held again

Safe until the next overflow

Days pass

Situation remains stable

Trust enters back in

Once again contained

When all seems well

Capacity is again breached

Overflow occurs

Sharing starts anew

Some destruction

New life begins, cycle repeats

Drifting

Enjoying the slow ride down stream

    Passing through the forest............ as in a dream

          Ripples in the water slap against the bow

Minor resistance against progress being made.......... on we float

Wish all life could pass by this slow

        ....but that idea will never flow

          The sun warms and the breeze cools

But alas like the hopes of fools

The day darkens, and this trip is at an end

          Well-worth the time....... my friend

Fear Reigns

World reacts to a crisis in different ways

Fear can be stirred to fanatical in a matter of days

Just keep bringing up all that can happen

Can make our once bright world blacken

Viruses and diseases will always be

And have been since the dawn of history

Fear and caution will help to ensure

Sanity until we can find a cure

Try to be social while still being alone

Letters and cards, until cure is known

Will have to be our connection

Fear or not, show some affection

Fear runs rampant and provokes

A demeanor in all that evokes

High anxiety and tension between

All who can and can't be seen

Charles Sahr

We will persevere through this scare

That threatens all things about which we care

When the battle is at last behind

We will need to be extra kind

For the enormous price it cost

In the many we have lost

Pain will be in many hearts

Until the healing starts

May smiles return sometime soon

Along with a joyous tune

We need each other near

So, we can put to rest our fear

Hidden Scars

Pain arrives in many ways

It can last for many days

Scars form on the outside

and on the inside

Visible scars heal overtime

Serving as reminders of a place in time

Hidden scars take longer to heal

Hanging on refusing to forget the ordeal

Each cure that is tried

Makes the situation better outside

Inside a different story

For there is no healing glory

Charles Sahr

Problems can be masked for a spell

Then all at once it can go to hell

Common sense would seem to say

They can beat this pain one day

However, that is often not the case

And many return to the same place

Time after time though they try to depart

It lingers on and seems locked into their heart

So, what does one do to push past?

Too frequently, once they realize at last

That each day will always be a fight

They decide to close the door and take flight

So, they at last find inner peace

For those behind pain will increase

A Graceful View

Some feel anger, others frustration

A few just are praying for their salvation

One must understand this was their choice

In that moment you had no voice

Though it hurts and you wish it were not so

You must come to terms and let them go.

Charles Sahr

Hurry

Darting to and fro

Never allowing a pause

Ahead or behind?

Perhaps better said

Is progress being made or

Just keeping busy

Too active to know

Whether or not effort works

Or how to enjoy

So, life passes by

Where to next? No answer but

It seems time to rest

Forward

Days blend into each other

Seamless transition

That ties the ribbon round

The package that is life

Charles Sahr

Tip tap

Anxiously awaiting

Hoping for good news

Tip tap

What is taking so long?

Seems like forever.

Tip tap

Finally, a reply

So good or bad?

What no decision

How can that be?

Tip tap

Well hopefully soon

A solution.

Tip tap

Tired of waiting

Time to move on

Tip tap

Or is it,

Time to go?

Tip Tap

Grace

Is it gone from life?

Seems all have a point to prove

Hate burns in their hearts

All have a complaint

For life is not fair

Those with grace adapt

Those with just anger

Vent and show hatred to all

And same returns

Wish they had the grace

To proceed ahead in life

As one, who sees love

Often, we will fail

Success comes to all in time

No matter your lot

Charles Sahr

Savor your moments

Our time here is limited

Then you will be judged

Not on what you did

But on how many you helped

Along the journey

Silence

Silence has many forms

It can bring terror at night

And calm in the day

So, is it golden?

Hoping time will clear that up

Answer split in two

Yes, when reading book

No, when you can't hear your heart

Beating in your chest

In summary it

Is good when you need to rest

Bad when you don't

Solo

Alone and apart

Wandering thru life solo

Not an easy task

Some find a partner

Sharing life much more fun

Now beauty is seen

Time steals them away

Now the journey seems rougher

Than it did before

Tears come quickly now

Until that long-awaited day

When reunited at last

Who Made Me, Me?

Not an easy feat to determine

Because so many played a part

Each had a role in making me

And each holds a place in my heart

Mom taught me how to love

And how to hang on to your dreams

Even though they might seem far above

What you believe you can reach

Dad taught me how to work

And how to treat other people right

He helped many along his journey

Often working on well into the night

Grandma was a giving soul

Not graced with great wealth

Her blessed and simple goal

Was to give her gifts baked with love

Charles Sahr

Grandpa was a humorous man

Who smiled, most of the time

He blessed me with the gift of laughter

When I think of him, I smile every time

Others had a hand in making me

Each brought something to my heart

That still today lives on in me

To each, I owe a debt of gratitude

Thanks for the love you shared with me

Along my journey thru this life

I learned a lot from each of thee

And I use it all, when dealing with strife

That comes with each and everyday

You trained me well, and thanks for all the love

Because of you, I start each day the old way

With a prayer and a thank you to the one above

Family Legacy

All families have one thing

That sets them apart

In mine, it was Christmas baking

My grandma's baked cookies

Mom and Dad followed suit

Mom had many recipes

Dad only two

I loved it then and now

The aroma in the kitchen

Was sweet, making our mouths

Water in anticipation

Mom made the cookies

That required decorating

At one time or another

All twelve of her children helped

Dad made his cookies solo

Charles Sahr

I passed this tradition down

To my children

Spending many nights

Decorating, mixing and baking

At one point, fifteen different kinds

Almost too much to handle

So, I had to cut down my list

It hurt, but I added some back in

Now I make the ones

My children or grandchildren like

Of course, I still add one or two

Just to keep it different

In general, I have a shorter list

I miss the days when all

Gathered round the table

But when the aroma is there, they are too

A Graceful View

Mom has been gone for years

Dad is no longer able

To participate

But when I start to decorate

I still feel Mom's hand

Reaching for my little hand

To guide it to the sprinkles

And the colored icing

I pray this baking continues

To future generations

It is truly about more than

just baking cookies

So, much more than that

It is about the precious time

Spent with family

Creating a family Legacy.

V.
RENEWAL

NEVER DONE

Days come, and days go

But we, all know

One day will be our last

Drifting away into the past

Will anyone remember my smile

Or what I did every once in awhile

Memory is all we become

After we succumb

No coming back for another act in the play

Just on to the place we hope and pray

Where we meet one's that passed before

I pray they open wide that door

Which separates death from life

Ending all worries and strife

If by chance that world does not exist

I hope and pray that my memory will persist

Charles Sahr

Forgive–Forget

Two sides of one dish,

Each important.

Heart controls one

Mind the other

Separate handles

Of the same plate

All share a single wish

Each important.

Letting go of one

And reducing the other

Different candles

Each guarding the gate

Forgive is possible.

With that one can live,

But how to forget?

Forgive and the sin

Is gone.

A Graceful View

Memory however remains,

And the sin retained.

So, it is not possible,

But we can still live

Just not forget.

Never give in

Though it lives on

Moved to the background

But as always, retained.

Charles Sahr

Always In My Heart

Perfectly living in an imperfect world,

Dealing with the trials of life

Positively and compassionately

Ever looking forward.

No problem too large or small

To eliminate and conquer

Faith, Love and Hope always

Part of your being.

No one ever a stranger

Left alone in the dark

You rarely confronted

And always consoled

A servant heart displayed

In darkness and light

A beacon of hope

In a sea of turmoil

A Graceful View

Always the teacher

During your stay

We've learned from you

To follow His way

Charles Sahr

Honor And Respect

Two words that should always be paired

And should also always be shared

With any and all that you meet

Sometimes this is easy, sometimes a feat

Honor thy family and all that they bring

Good, bad or indifferent, it is everything

Show respect to all,according to his plan

Equally to each woman and man

No one should be treated different

Even if it seems apparent

They are not giving anything in return

That is their choice, maybe one day they'll turn

And start to follow his way

Or at least that is what we pray

Never waver from the path of right

Even if staying there takes all of your might

A Graceful View

Your duty is not to change their ways

But to show them how one should walk always

Patience will help you make the point clear

Actions speak louder than words here

Shipmate

Days spent aboard

Seem to pass slowly by

Then in an instant, gone

Into our memory

We shared more than the sea

Laughter, friendship, and more.

We worked round the clock

Wrote constant letters home

Keeping each other going

When our limits were exceeded

We had each other's back

For we were all missing home

Now as I look back

I realize what true friends I made

On a hunk of steel

Sailing the endless sea

We were men, who gave of themselves

To proudly serve this country

Not in a foxhole

A Graceful View

But on a ship at sea

Proud to have walked this path

With heroes I can still recall

What a journey we shared

On that hunk of steel

A Moment

Once gone no return

So, savor each moment

Plan for tomorrow

And hope for many more days

Do not waste or burn

Each second sent

For like a flame it will go

And be lost in the maze

Memory only holds for a while

And soon all is lost

From that moment shared

With the one you love

Replay all in your head and smile

For no matter the cost

That precious moment shared

Was a gift from above

Blessings

Always will bend my knee to pray,

Thanking the Lord for my three.

No matter what happens

Three Blessings will always be.

Two sons and a daughter to raise,

Each a blessing sent from above.

Whatever transpires throughout my days,

I shall always feel the Lord's Love.

They each brought me pleasure,

I have been most enriched by the three.

I shall forever treasure,

Each and every one of thee.

When my days are over,

And their tears subside.

Hopefully they'll discover,

A part of me still inside.

Charles Sahr

To My Love

How blest I was

To meet you by pure chance

In what was my darkest hour

My spirit defeated

Then in an instant

After meeting you

My heart beat a little faster

And my smile returned

Thank the Lord above

For placing you into my life

It is our journey now

Since you and I are one

I am a better man

Than before we met

Not perfect by any means

But better and happier by far.

Calming

They snuggle up to you

Warming you and your heart up

You say they are pets

But they are so much more

They help you through the rough times

Just by snuggling

Smiles they bring make everything

Seem a little easier

They make your life better

In a number of ways

Some are easy to identify

Others not so much

Charles Sahr

Precious

Moment of your birth

Watching you go off to school,

Your graduation day

Teaching you to drive

Celebrating your wedding

Birth of our grandchild

All the moments shared

Between you and I are kept

Safe inside my heart

When my time is up

I pray those moments will be

Things that bring me back

Know this too my child

You will never walk alone

For my love is there

Believe In You

You are one of a kind

No duplicate will you find

You have always brought a smile

With your unique and special style

Your future will exceed your dreams

Though at the moment it seems

That day is so very far away

Trust me, it will come one day

Charles Sahr

Never Quit

Move on forward

Through storms

That beset your path

Hold true always

Come on toward

Emerging light

Showing the way

To continue on

Will success be

Time will tell

Whether or not

Battle is won

Breathe free

And move on

For each day

Brings small victory

How To

How to move forward

When life seems to fall apart

And your spirit aches

Look outside yourself

Help someone in dire need

Make your aches ease

A simple fact that

Love is how you stay alive

Simple and so true

Date of Creation

SPRING

Harbinger Of Spring, 6 Dec 2019
Layers, 14 Jan 2020
Just A Prayer Away, 25 Oct 2019
Trust In Us, 29 Aug 2012
One Day, 27 Mar 2019
All Is Well, 2 Dec 2019
Admired, 24 Nov 2020
Pitter Patter, 18 May 2017
Behind The Glass, 15 Apr 2019
Break A Rule, 28 Apr 2020
A Birthday Wish, 18 Mar 2020
Child Of Mine, 7 Nov 2019
Zig Zag, 10 May 2019
The Smile Returns, 30 Jan 2020
To Those Lost, 31 Mar 2020
Doorstep, 21 May 2019
Wren, 23 Oct 2019
Intense, 8 Apr 19
From Dust To Dust, 8 Apr 2020
Time Will Tell, 13 Jan 2020

SUMMER

Summer Daze, 10 Jul 2019
Beach House, 15 Jul 2019
Blank Canvas, 16 Jul 2019
Crayons, 27 Mar 2019
Creativity, 30 Jul 2020
Composed, 22 Jul 2020

AUTUMN

WINTER

It Brings Me Back, 26 Aug 2019
Too Quiet, 16 Mar 2020
What Was Once, 5 Sept 2012
In The Silence Of The Night, 6 Nov 2019
Time, 9 Jan 2019
Overflow, 9 Dec 2019
Drifting, 18 Apr 2019
Fear Reigns, 16 Mar 2020
Hidden Scars, 16 Sept 2019
Hurry, 5 Dec 2019
Forward, 11 Jan 2024
Tip Tap, 10 Apr 2019
Grace, 12 Dec 2019
Silence, 12 Sept 2019
Solo, 5 Dec 2019
Who Made Me, Me?, 26 Nov 2019
Family Legacy, 1 Mar 2020

RENEWAL

NEVER DONE, 20 June 2019
Forgive-Forget, 9 Apr 2019
Always In My Heart, 12 Jun 2014
Honor And Respect, 5 Sept 2019
Shipmate, 27 Aug 2020
A Moment, 25 Jul 2019
Blessings, 10 Sept 2012
To My Love, 14 Feb 2020
Calming, 28 Jan 2024
Precious, 30 Oct 2019
Believe In You, 30 Sept 2019
Never Quit, 12 Apr 2019
How To, 15 Feb 2020